LEARN ABOUT

The OLYMPIC GAMES

HISTORY
2

OLYMPIC SPORTS
12

THE PARALYMPIC GAMES
20

ATHLETES
24

BRAZIL IN THE GAMES
34

QUIZ
36

HISTORY

Ancient Times

The first Olympic Games are held in Olympia, in ancient Greece.

776 BC

The Olympic Games are abolished in Greece.

393 AD

Rio de Janeiro is the first South American city to host the Olympic Games.

2020

The Tokyo Olympic Games are postponed until 2021, due to the COVID-19 pandemic, but the name Tokyo 2020 is maintained. It is the first time the Olympics have been postponed.

2016

2010

The first Youth Olympic Games take place in Singapore.

1988

The host city starts to stage both the Summer Olympic and the Paralympic Games.

Discobolus. Famous Greek statue by Myron of Eleutherae, from around 455 BC. It shows an athlete throwing a discus. His body is athletic and shows his strength, but his face is smooth. The original statue no longer exists, but a few Roman copies in bronze and marble have survived to the present day.

Several editions of the Olympic Games were influenced by the political context of the time when they occurred.

War and peace

*In the 1964 Tokyo Olympics, Japanese athlete **Yoshinori Sakai** lit the Olympic flame.*

1920

In Antwerp, white doves were released for the first time during the opening ceremony of the Olympic Games as a symbol of peace after World War I. Nevertheless, some countries involved in the war were not allowed to take part in the Games.

1936

In Berlin, African-American athlete **Jesse Owens** won four gold medals and set world records in athletics, defeating German athlete Luz Long in the long jump event. It has been said that dictator Adolf Hitler left the stadium just after that to avoid congratulating the winner. In spite of this, the two athletes became friends and Long received a posthumous medal from the IOC for the Olympic spirit he had demonstrated, accepting defeat at that historic moment. The Berlin Olympics have other stories related to the Nazi government: the call for boycott by Jewish athletes, actions to disguise violent police interventions, tricks to get German athletes to win, etc.

1940 and 1944

The Games were canceled due to World War II.

1964

Japanese athlete **Yoshinori Sakai** lit the Olympic flame in Tokyo. He was born in Hiroshima on August 6th, 1945, the day the United States dropped a nuclear bomb on the city and destroyed it. His participation in the Olympics represented the reconstruction of Japan and was a symbolic call for peace after the two World Wars.

1968

In Mexico City, African-American athletes **Tommie Smith** and **John Carlos** protested against racism. After receiving their award on the podium, they raised black-gloved fists and kept them raised until the end of the American national anthem. As a consequence, they were expelled from the Games. Their compatriots Lee Evans, Larry James, and Ronald Freeman protested in a similar way: they received their medals while wearing black berets.

> In ancient Greece, an Olympiad was the period of four years between the competitions. Nowadays, the word "Olympic" refers to the name of the sports event.

1972

In Munich, nine members of the Israeli delegation were taken hostage and then killed by an Arab terrorist group which demanded the release of two hundred Arab prisoners. Two other Israeli athletes, a policeman, and five terrorists were also killed. The Games were interrupted for 34 hours. This was the saddest and most violent edition of the history of the Olympic Games.

1980

The United States and 60 other delegations decided to boycott the Moscow Olympic Games as a response to the Soviet invasion of Afghanistan (which was then supported by the USA). Athletes of those countries were disappointed to see their hard work and preparation wasted. In return, various communist countries boycotted the 1984 Los Angeles Games.

In subsequent editions of the Games, the countries involved in conflicts agreed on a ceasefire so as to make it easier for their athletes to take part in the Olympic Games. However, until 1988 there had been some countries that still boycotted the Games for political reasons.

The Berlin Olympic Games are canceled due to World War I, but the edition is considered in the official count as the 6th Olympic Games.

The Olympic flag with the interlocking rings is raised and athletes take the Olympic oath for the first time.

The first Winter Olympic Games are held in Chamonix, France.

The tradition of lighting and extinguishing the Olympic flame starts in Amsterdam.

1916 **1920** **1924** **1928**

The duration of the Games is reduced from 79 to 16 days.

1932

1936

The Olympic flame is transported from Olympia (Greece) to the host city (Berlin) for the first time.

1940

The Helsinki Olympic Games are canceled due to World War II, but this edition is officially recorded as the 12th Olympic Games.

1944

The London Olympic Games are canceled due to World War II, but this edition is also officially recorded, being considered the 13th Olympic Games.

1960

The first Paralympic Games are held in Rome.

1956

The Games are broadcast on television for the first time during the Winter Olympics, held in Cortina d'Ampezzo, Italy.

3

Modern Age

ench baron
erre de Coubertin
863-1937)
poses to reinstate
e Olympic Games
ancient times
d founds the
ernational Olympic
ommittee (IOC).

The first Olympic Games of the Modern Age are held in Athens, Greece.

Women compete in the Olympics for the first time.

The three best competitors are awarded the gold, silver, and bronze medals for the first time.

Greece organizes an extraordinary international edition of the Olympics in Athens. However, the IOC does not recognize it as an official event.

Pierre de Coubertin creates the symbol of the five interlocking rings on a white field to represent the five continents and all their nations.

1894 **1896** **1900** **1904** **1906** **1913**

THE GAMES THROUGH TIME

The Olympic Games were created in ancient Greece in 776 BC. At that time, they were directly related to the worship of the god Zeus and were held in the city of Olympia. Competitions lasted 5 days and included running, jumping, throwing, fighting, shooting, equestrian events, and pentathlon. Athletes came from various Greek cities and women were prohibited from participating. In 393 AD, Roman emperor Theodosius I banned the Games, which were only reinstated in 1896.

1978
The Olympic Charter (originally written by Coubertin in 1898) is published in Switzerland. The document sets the principles, rules, and guidelines adopted by the IOC for the Olympic Games. It also presents the values associated with the Games: friendship, mutual understanding, equality, solidarity, and fair play.

'88 SEOUL PARALYMPICS

Host cities

The host city election process starts nine years before the Games. It has two stages: application and candidacy. In the second stage, cities must present a number of documents describing their proposals and demonstrating their ability to organize such an important event. Among many requirements, host cities must:

➤ be able to receive over 10,000 athletes and their delegations, national and international media professionals (nearly the same number as that of athletes!), and local and foreign volunteers (about 60,000!);

➤ provide appropriate sports facilities for the competitions to be held in;

➤ have land and air transportation, lodging (including the Olympic Village), tourism infrastructure, and, above all, high level of security;

➤ have comfortable weather conditions during the time of the Games: neither too hot nor too cold;

➤ be located at a suitable altitude, given that high altitudes impose difficulties on breathing and limit athletes' performance.

The authority responsible for this election is the International Olympic Committee (IOC). Being a host city for the Olympic Games involves making financial and technological investments in tourism and culture, both in the host city itself and in the country as a whole.

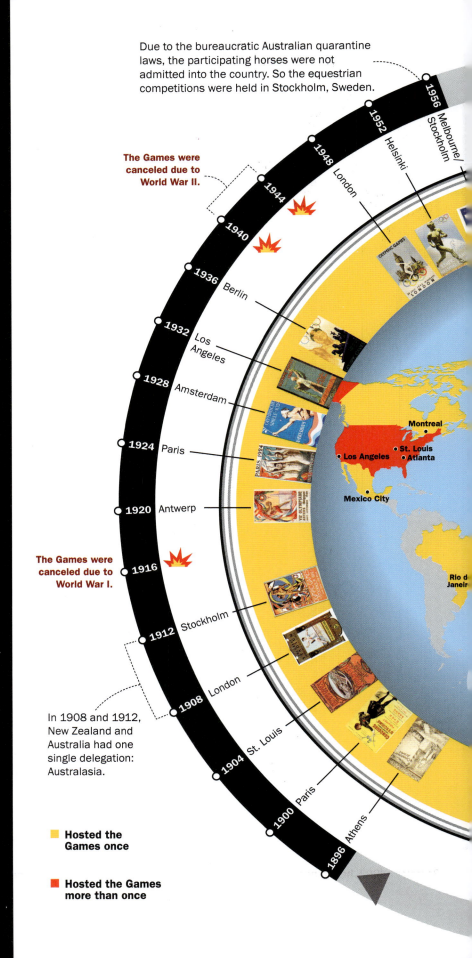

Due to the bureaucratic Australian quarantine laws, the participating horses were not admitted into the country. So the equestrian competitions were held in Stockholm, Sweden.

The Games were canceled due to World War II.

The Games were canceled due to World War I.

In 1908 and 1912, New Zealand and Australia had one single delegation: Australasia.

■ Hosted the Games once
■ Hosted the Games more than once

THE WINTER OLYMPIC GAMES

The first Winter Sports Week took place in Chamonix, France, in 1924. Two years later, it was officially recognized as the first edition of the Winter Olympic Games.

Until 1992, these Games were held in the same year as the Summer Games. Since 1994, in Lillehammer, Norway, an official calendar was established for the Winter Games. They began to be held once every four years, alternating with the Summer Games.

In these Games, all the competitions are held on ice or snow.

○ Games held in the same year as the Summer Games

- **1924** Chamonix **FRANCE** — First edition of the Winter Olympic Games.
- **1928** St. Moritz **SWITZERLAND**
- **1932** Lake Placid **UNITED STATES**
- **1936** Garmisch-Partenkirchen **GERMANY**
- **1940** / **1944** The Games were canceled due to World War II.
- **1948** St. Moritz **SWITZERLAND**
- **1952** Oslo **NORWAY**
- **1956** Cortina d'Ampezzo **ITALY**
- **1960** Squaw Valley **UNITED STATES** — Insufficient snow in the host city caused organizers to bring blocks of ice from the mountains to allow the competitions to take place.
- **1964** Innsbruck **AUSTRIA**
- **1968** Grenoble **FRANCE** — Due to high temperatures, the luge and bobsleigh competitions did not get to the final stage. Results from the third round were considered final.
- **1972** Sapporo **JAPAN**

8

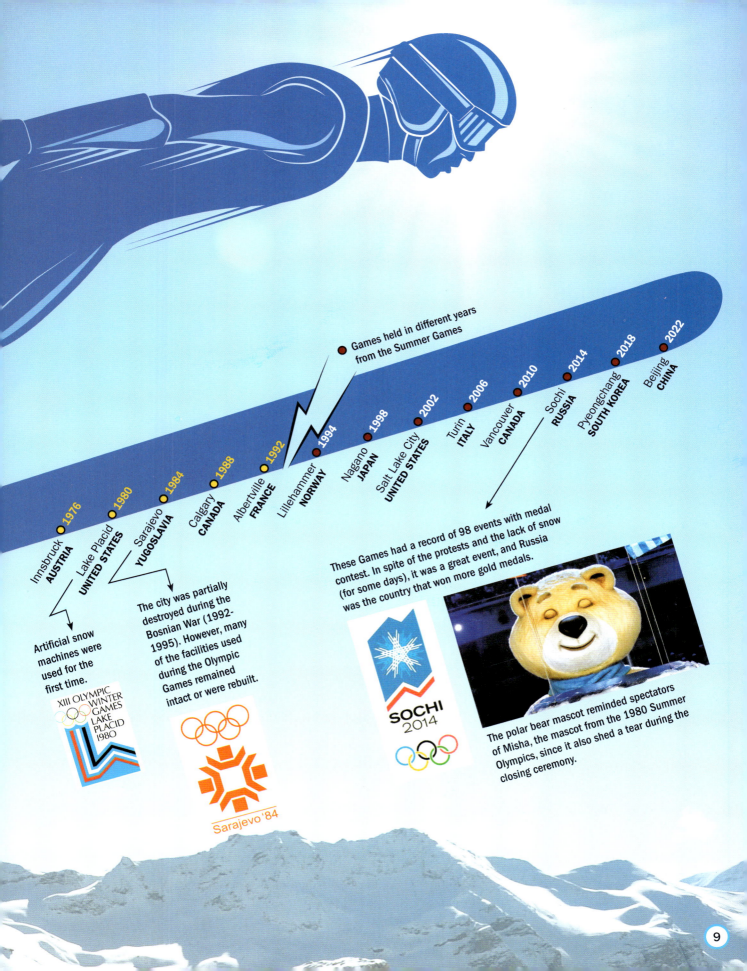

- 1976 Innsbruck **AUSTRIA**
- 1980 Lake Placid **UNITED STATES** — Artificial snow machines were used for the first time.
- 1984 Sarajevo **YUGOSLAVIA** — The city was partially destroyed during the Bosnian War (1992-1995). However, many of the facilities used during the Olympic Games remained intact or were rebuilt.
- 1988 Calgary **CANADA**
- 1992 Albertville **FRANCE**
- 1994 Lillehammer **NORWAY** — Games held in different years from the Summer Games
- 1998 Nagano **JAPAN**
- 2002 Salt Lake City **UNITED STATES**
- 2006 Turin **ITALY**
- 2010 Vancouver **CANADA**
- 2014 Sochi **RUSSIA** — These Games had a record of 98 events with medal contest. In spite of the protests and the lack of snow (for some days), it was a great event, and Russia was the country that won more gold medals.
- 2018 Pyeongchang **SOUTH KOREA**
- 2022 Beijing **CHINA**

The polar bear mascot reminded spectators of Misha, the mascot from the 1980 Summer Olympics, since it also shed a tear during the closing ceremony.

9

The Youth Olympic Games

"Learning to know, learning to do, learning to be, and learning to live together."

In addition to the Summer and Winter Olympics and the Paralympic Games, there are the **Youth Olympic Games**, which take place every four years exclusively for athletes aged 15 to 18.

These games were created by physician and former athlete **Jacques Rogge** in 2001, when he was chair of the International Olympic Committee. His goal was to motivate young people to practice sports in order to improve their health and fight obesity in children and youth. Another goal of the proposal was to strengthen the role of Physical Education, which had been removed from the curriculum in some schools, thus affecting the values stimulated by sports and the Olympic spirit. He defended that every edition of the Games should promote sessions of the **Culture and Education Program**.

The sports that are part of the Youth Olympic Games are generally the same as those of the traditional Games, but not all the sports and disciplines are contested, and some are adapted. Also, mixed teams, with both boys and girls, are allowed.

Former and current Olympic athletes offer courses, workshops, and talks on topics such as Olympic values, social responsibility, skills development, communication and well-being, and healthy lifestyles, besides career planning and the environment.

A brief history of the Youth Olympic Games

Summer Games

- **2010 SINGAPORE** Singapore
- **2014 NANJING** China
- **2018 BUENOS AIRES** Argentina
- **2022 DAKAR** Senegal

Lausanne 2020 Mascot: Yodli

Winter Games

- **2012 INNSBRUCK** Austria
- **2016 LILLEHAMMER** Norway
- **2020 LAUSANNE** Switzerland

Scan this QR code to learn more about the **history of the Olympic Games**.
http://mod.lk/olygame

OLYMPIC SPORTS

IN EACH EDITION OF THE OLYMPIC GAMES, sports are added or removed from the official list. This depends on factors such as the number of athletes, their level of professionalism, their federations, etc.

Some sports have made several attempts since the beginning of the Games to be considered an Olympic sport, but still haven't succeeded. This is the case of pigeon shooting (prohibited in order to protect birds), balloon racing, cannon shooting, donkey racing, kite flying, fishing, and billiards. Other sports, such as stone lifting and rope climbing, despite their eccentricity, have made the list, but only for a while.

Some sports that are no longer part of the Olympics include boating, tug-of-war, cricket, croquet, palm game, lacrosse, Basque pelota, polo, racquetball, and roque.

Sports such as bowling, futsal, squash, speed skating, and wakeboarding are trying to enter or return to the list of official Olympic sports.

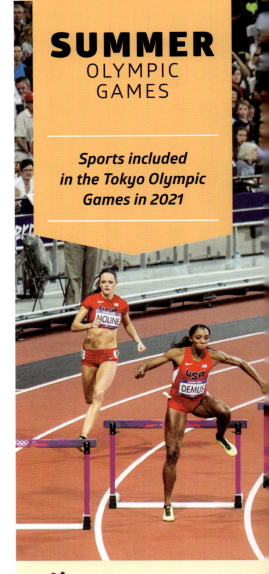

SUMMER OLYMPIC GAMES

Sports included in the Tokyo Olympic Games in 2021

ATHLETICS

Athletics is the most traditional sport in the Olympics; it can be traced back to ancient Greece. The disciplines included in athletics are track and field (running, jumping, and throwing), road running (**marathon**), and racewalking events (race walk), as well as combined disciplines such as decathlon for men and heptathlon for women.

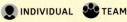

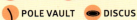

HURDLE RACE

- Exclusive **pictograms** were developed to officially represent the Olympic disciplines. They were first used in 1948 and, since then, have been reinvented in each edition. The pictograms used here are the ones for the Tokyo 2020 Olympic Games.
- The Latin phrase *Citius, Altius, Fortius* ("faster, higher, stronger") represents the athletics disciplines running, jumping, and throwing. In 1894, Pierre de Coubertin proposed that these words be the motto of the Games.
- The **discipline** came from a Greek legend: the Greek athlete and soldier Pheidippides was sent from the plain of Marathon to the city of Athens to announce the Greeks' victory over the Persians in the First Greco-Persian War. It is said that he died from exhaustion. Athens is 40 km away from Marathon, which is the approximate distance marathoners run in the Modern Age.

BADMINTON
It is a very popular sport in Southeast Asia and, because of the number of people who play it, it is one of the world's most popular sports. It became an Olympic sport in Barcelona 1992 and, since then, Asian countries have won the most medals.

👤 SINGLE　👥 DOUBLE
🏸 RACKET　🏸 SHUTTLECOCK

BASKETBALL
In 1904, basketball was introduced as a sport during the St. Louis Games. Back then, the baskets were similar to those used for picking peaches, but with holes. Basketball baskets have evolved and, in 1906, they started being built with metal rings. Basketball became an official Olympic sport in Berlin 1936. In Tokyo 2020, 3x3 basketball will be included in the Olympic Games for the first time. It developed from street basketball and is played on half a court, with teams shooting into the same hoop.

👥 TEAM　🏀 BASKET　● BALL

BOXING
This sport has been part of the Games since the ancient Olympics, but it was included for the first time in the Modern Age in St. Louis 1904. Since then, it has been part of all Olympic Games, except for Stockholm 1912, because a law forbade this sport on Swedish soil.

👤 INDIVIDUAL　🥊 GLOVES

CANOE SLALOM
Athletes use light canoes or kayaks because they are more resistant to white waters. They are smaller than the ones used in speed sailing in order to make maneuvers more agile, allowing athletes to pass the mandatory gates (which are around 18 to 25).

👤 SINGLE
🛶 PADDLE　● KAYAK　— CANOE

CANOE SPRINT
Long and aerodynamic kayaks or canoes are used, since they are more appropriate for calm waters.

👤 SINGLE　👥 DOUBLE　👥 TEAM
🛶 PADDLE　● KAYAK　— CANOE

CYCLING BMX
BMX means "bicycle motocross". In Tokyo 2020, besides the speed race, the program will feature a freestyle event for the first time.

👤 INDIVIDUAL　🚴 BICYCLE　⛑ HELMET

CYCLING MOUNTAIN BIKE
"Tracks" in this sport are the land itself, with its ups and downs and outdoor challenges. Bicycles are resistant, but not heavy: they weigh no more than 9 kg.

👤 INDIVIDUAL　🚴 BICYCLE　⛑ HELMET

13

CYCLING ROAD
Athletes use bicycles made of carbon weighing up to 6.8 kg. Currently, bikes must have no more than 20 gears.
 INDIVIDUAL BICYCLE

 CYCLING TRACK
Competitions are held at velodromes, where tracks are made of wood.
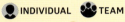 INDIVIDUAL TEAM
 BICYCLE HELMET

 MARATHON SWIMMING
This discipline was held for the first time in Beijing 2008. Athletes must swim 10 km in open waters.
 INDIVIDUAL  RIVER OR SEA

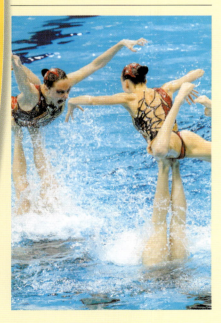

ARTISTIC SWIMMING
It is an exclusively female discipline, in which a duet or a team performs a choreography that includes highly coordinated movements in the water.
 DUET TEAM  SWIMMING POOL

 SWIMMING
It is one of the oldest sports in the world and has been part of all the Modern Olympic Games. At the beginning, this discipline was held in open waters, but after 1908 it started to be held in swimming pools.
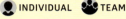 INDIVIDUAL TEAM
SWIMMING POOL

 WATER POLO
This was the first collective Olympic sport. It was played for the first time in Paris 1900.
 TEAM SWIMMING POOL
 BALL GOAL

 DIVING
The competitions include 3- and 10-meter jumps from platforms or springboards. Since Sydney 2000, there have been events that include a team of two athletes who perform synchronized jumps.
INDIVIDUAL DOUBLE
SWIMMING POOL PLATFORM
SPRINGBOARD

 FENCING
It has been part of the Games since the first Modern Olympics. There are three weapon categories: foil, saber, and épée.
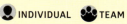 INDIVIDUAL TEAM
 SWORD MASK

 FOOTBALL
In order to participate in the Olympics, players must be no older than 23, except for three members of the team. There are no age restrictions for the women's tournament.
 TEAM BALL GOAL

 ARTISTIC GYMNASTICS
A traditional discipline in ancient times, this sport has been part of the Games since its first edition in the Modern Age. Women's categories are: uneven bars, beam, vault, and floor. Men's categories are: rings, vault, parallel bars, horizontal bar, pommel horse, and floor.
INDIVIDUAL TEAM BARS
POMMEL HORSE RINGS

 TRAMPOLINE
This appeared as a form of training for trapeze artists and astronauts. This discipline was included in the Olympic Games for the first time in Sydney 2000.
 INDIVIDUAL TRAMPOLINE

RHYTHMIC GYMNASTICS WITH CLUBS

 **RHYTHMIC GYMNASTICS**
This is a women's discipline only. Four out of five apparatuses are used in each competition.
 INDIVIDUAL GROUP ROPE
HOOP BALL RIBBON CLUBS

GOLF

This sport returned to the games in Rio 2016, after an absence of over 100 years. Athletes play four rounds of 18 holes, totaling 72 holes.

 INDIVIDUAL  CLUBS AND BALL

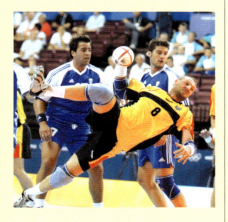

 **HANDBALL**

This sport is known as "football with hands".

 TEAM   BALL   GOAL

 EQUESTRIAN/ DRESSAGE

This sport can be traced back to ancient Greece. The horse's discipline, obedience, and grace are evaluated. In equestrian competitions, there are mixed teams: women and men compete together.

 INDIVIDUAL   TEAM   HORSE

 EQUESTRIAN/ EVENTING

It started as a competition among the military, and until 1948 only officers could compete. It is called "the equestrian triathlon" because it includes dressage, cross-country, and show jumping.

 INDIVIDUAL   TEAM
 HORSE OBSTACLE

EQUESTRIAN/JUMPING

This competition includes a course of 8 to 12 obstacles, such as fence and water jump.

 TEAM   HORSE   OBSTACLE

15

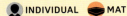 ### WRESTLING
It is the second oldest sport in the Olympics. There are two styles in wrestling: the Greco-Roman style (wrestlers only use their arms and trunk) and freestyle (besides their arms and trunk, wrestlers can use their legs).

 INDIVIDUAL MAT

 ### KARATE
Karate will appear for the first time as an Olympic sport in Tokyo 2020. Two events are on the program: kata (which exercises power and speed) and kumite (which aims at touching the opponent by using punches and kicks).

 INDIVIDUAL MAT

FENCING

WEIGHTLIFTING
There are two types of competition: the "snatch" (the athlete lifts the weight up to their head and holds it for two seconds) and the "clean and jerk" (the athlete lifts the weight up to their shoulder and then up to their head).

 INDIVIDUAL BARBELL

 ### SKATEBOARDING
The sport will feature at the Olympic Games for the first time in Tokyo 2020. The competition will include two events: park (having bowls and pools with ramps and course bends) and street (with stairs, curbs, rails, and slopes).

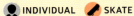 INDIVIDUAL SKATE

 ### SPORT CLIMBING
In 2014, the sport was part of the Youth Olympic Games Sports Lab initiative in Nanjing, China. It will feature at the Olympic Games for the first time in Tokyo 2020. Athletes will compete in three disciplines: bouldering, lead climbing, and speed climbing.

 INDIVIDUAL CLIMBING WALL

 ### MODERN PENTATHLON
This includes fencing, freestyle swimming, show jumping, and a final combined event of pistol shooting and cross-country run.

 INDIVIDUAL SWORD SWIMMING POOL HORSE FIELD PISTOL

 ### BASEBALL/SOFTBALL
At the Olympic Games, baseball is played only by men. It was first contested at the Games in Barcelona 1992 and it will return in Tokyo 2020. The same thing will happen to softball, which is played only by women at the Olympic Games. The two main differences between these sports are the pitching style and the size of the field.

 TEAM BAT BALL

 ### HOCKEY
India is the leader in hockey. The Indian men's team won in every Olympics edition from 1928 to 1956.

 TEAM STICK BALL

 ### JUDO
Judo means "gentle way".

 SINGLE MAT

 ### SURFING
Surfing will feature at the Olympic Games for the first time in Tokyo 2020. Participants will use shortboards in the competition.

 INDIVIDUAL SURFBOARD

ROWING

This sport has been part of the Olympic Games since Athens 1896, but in that year the competition had to be canceled due to bad weather.

- SINGLE
- PAIR
- TEAM
- OAR
- BOAT

RUGBY

This sport was included in the Olympic Games thanks to Pierre de Coubertin, who was a huge rugby fan. It was only included as a discipline in the years of 1900, 1908, 1920, and 1924, but returned to the Games in Rio 2016.

- TEAM
- BALL

TAEKWONDO

The name of this Korean martial art means "the way of the foot and the hand".

- INDIVIDUAL
- TRUNK PROTECTOR
- HEAD PROTECTOR

TENNIS

In this sport, mixed pairs are allowed.

- SINGLE
- DOUBLE
- RACKET
- BALL

TABLE TENNIS

Table tennis started in England as a classy after-dinner game. It became very popular in China and, for this reason, it is the sport with more fans than any other around the world. During a match, the ball can reach a speed of 150 km/h.

- SINGLE
- DOUBLE
- TEAM
- RACKET
- BALL
- TABLE

ARCHERY

Archers can only use recurve bows to compete, which makes the competition even harder for them. The target is 70 m away from the athlete and arrows can reach a speed of 240 km/h.

- INDIVIDUAL
- TEAM
- BOW AND ARROW
- TARGET

SHOOTING

Competitors use pistols and rifles. Nowadays, targets are circle-shaped and do not include images of animals or people in order to avoid the relation between this sport and violence. To increase their aim, shooters control their heartbeats and only shoot between one heartbeat and another.

- INDIVIDUAL
- TEAM
- WEAPON
- TARGET

TRIATHLON

This is a resistance sport and it became part of the Olympics in Sydney 2000. It includes a 1.5-km swim, a 40-km cycle, and a 10-km run, in this order.

- INDIVIDUAL
- TEAM
- SEA
- BICYCLE
- ROAD

SAILING

Brazil has won 18 medals in this sport: 7 gold medals, 3 silver medals, and 8 bronze medals.

- ONE-PERSON
- TWO-PERSON
- SAIL BOAT

BEACH VOLLEYBALL

This is one of the sports in which Brazil has excelled in the Olympic Games.

- DOUBLE
- BALL
- BEACH

VOLLEYBALL

Brazil also excels in volleyball. In Los Angeles 1984, a sky ball serve was performed for the first time by Brazilian player Bernard Rajzman. This serve would become known as "Star Trek".

- TEAM
- BALL

17

WINTER OLYMPIC GAMES

Sports included in the Pyeongchang 2018 Olympic Games

 BIATHLON
This discipline combines cross-country skiing and rifle shooting.
INDIVIDUAL TEAM POLES RIFLE SKI

 **BOBSLEIGH**
This is a sled sport.
TWO-MAN FOUR-MAN SLED

 **NORDIC COMBINED**
This is a discipline that combines 10 km of cross-country skiing and ski jumping. It is a sport only for men.
INDIVIDUAL TEAM SKI

 ALPINE SKIING
It combines five types of events for women and for men.
INDIVIDUAL TEAM SKI SKI POLES

 CROSS-COUNTRY SKIING
INDIVIDUAL TEAM SKI POLES

 FREESTYLE SKIING
This combines five events for women and men.
INDIVIDUAL SKI POLES

 CURLING
Curling stones weigh around 20 kg.
DOUBLE TEAM STONE BROOM

 LUGE
It is one of the most dangerous winter sports.
SINGLE DOUBLE TEAM SLED

 **ICE HOCKEY**
TEAM STICK PUCK

18

FIGURE SKATING
This is the oldest winter sport. There are men-only and women-only events, as well as mixed events.

 INDIVIDUAL   PAIRS
TEAM SKATES

SHORT TRACK
INDIVIDUAL TEAM SKATES

SPEED SKATING
INDIVIDUAL TEAM SKATES

SKI JUMPING
It has been part of the Winter Olympic Games since its first edition.

  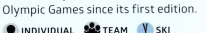
INDIVIDUAL TEAM SKI

Scan this QR code to learn more about **Olympic sports**.
http://mod.lk/olysport

SKELETON

INDIVIDUAL SLED

SNOWBOARD

INDIVIDUAL SNOWBOARD

American athlete **Marla Runyan**, who has less than 10% of her vision, was the first visually impaired person to compete in the Olympic and Paralympic Games. In Barcelona 1992, she won four gold medals and, in Atlanta 1996, two more: a gold and a silver medal.

The symbol of the **Paralympic Games** is called *agito*, which means "I move" in Latin.

Mandeville was the name of one of the mascots of the London 2012 Paralympic Games.

New Zealander archer **Neroli Fairhall** was the first paraplegic athlete who participated in the Olympic Games. This happened in 1984, in Los Angeles.

THE PARALYMPIC GAMES

IN 1948, IN STOKE MANDEVILLE, a village near London, a neurologist called Sir Ludwig Guttmann organized the first sporting event for World War II veterans who had been wounded, as part of their rehabilitation process. Twelve editions later, in Rome 1960, this competition became the Paralympic Games. Since 1988, the Paralympic Games are held in the same city that hosts the Summer Games, a few weeks after the Olympics have finished. They are also held in the same facilities, after some adaptations.

The word that defines the Paralympic Games is **overcome**. Athletes with congenital or acquired disabilities compete in different disciplines, according to their needs.

THE SUMMER PARALYMPIC GAMES

Sports included in the Tokyo 2020 Summer Paralympic Games

WHEELCHAIR BASKETBALL
This sport has been part of all editions of the Paralympic Games. Players are athletes who have a physical-motor disability.

TEAM · BASKET · BALL

BOCCIA
This sport is played by athletes who have a physical-motor disability.

INDIVIDUAL · PAIRS · TEAM · BALL

WHEELCHAIR FENCING
Three types of weapons are used in this competition: foil, saber, and épée. Athletes who have a locomotor disability can compete in this discipline.

INDIVIDUAL · TEAM · SWORD · MASK

FOOTBALL 5-A-SIDE
It is played by athletes with visual impairments.

TEAM · BALL THAT RATTLES · GOAL

GOALBALL
It is played by visually impaired athletes.

TEAM · BALL THAT RATTLES · GOAL

POWERLIFTING
This sport is played by athletes who have a physical-motor disability.

INDIVIDUAL · BARBELL

EQUESTRIAN
It consists only of dressage events. Men and women compete together. In the Paralympic Games, horses also win medals. Athletes with physical-motor disabilities or visual impairments can participate in this event.

INDIVIDUAL · TEAM · HORSE

JUDO
Visually impaired athletes can compete in this discipline.

INDIVIDUAL · MAT

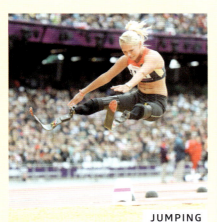

JUMPING

ATHLETICS
It consists of track events, such as sprints, middle- or long-distance runs (relay and marathon); field events, such as jumping and throwing; and combined sports, like pentathlon. Athletes with motor, sensory, or intellectual disabilities can participate.

INDIVIDUAL · TEAM · TRACK · HURDLES · DISCUS · POLE VAULT

The first Paralympic Games pictograms were introduced in Barcelona 1992.

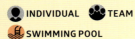 SWIMMING
Athletes with a physical-motor or intellectual disability, as well as those who are visually impaired, compete in this discipline.

👤 INDIVIDUAL 👥 TEAM
🏊 SWIMMING POOL

🚣 CANOE
This sport was included for the first time in Rio 2016. There are men's and women's events, as well as mixed events. Athletes with physical-motor disabilities compete in this discipline.

👤 SINGLE 👥 DOUBLE
 PADDLE CANOE KAYAK

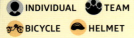 CYCLING
Athletes who have a physical disability or visual impairments can participate in this event.

👤 INDIVIDUAL 👥 TEAM
🚴 BICYCLE ⛑ HELMET

 BADMINTON
The sport will be part of the Paralympic Games for the first time in Tokyo 2020. It is played by athletes who have a physical-motor disability.

👤 SINGLE 👥 DOUBLE
🏸 RACKET SHUTTLECOCK

 WHEELCHAIR TENNIS
It is played by athletes who have a physical disability.

👤 SINGLE 👥 DOUBLE
🏸 RACKET ⚾ BALL

 TRIATHLON
This sport was included in the Paralympic Games for the first time in Rio 2016. It consists of three events: a 750-m swimming event, a 20-km cycling event and a 5-km athletic run. Athletes with physical-motor disabilities and visual impairments compete in this discipline.

👤 INDIVIDUAL 🌊 SEA
🚴 BICYCLE 🛣 ROAD

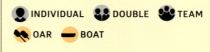 ROWING
Athletes who have a physical disability or visual impairments can participate in this discipline.

👤 INDIVIDUAL 👥👥 DOUBLE   TEAM
🏓 OAR 🚤 BOAT

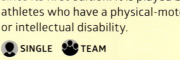 TABLE TENNIS
This is one of the sports that have been part of the Paralympic Games since its first edition. It is played by athletes who have a physical-motor or intellectual disability.

👤 SINGLE  TEAM
🏓 RACKET ⚾ BALL 🟰 TABLE

SITTING VOLLEYBALL
Athletes with physical-motor disabilities participate in this sport.

👥 TEAM ⚾ BALL

 TAEKWONDO
The sport will be part of the Paralympic Games for the first time in Tokyo 2020. It is played by athletes who have a physical-motor or intellectual disability.

👤 INDIVIDUAL 🛡 TRUNK PROTECTOR
⛑ HEAD PROTECTOR

 ARCHERY
Athletes with a physical-motor disability can participate in this event.

👤 INDIVIDUAL 👥 TEAM
🏹 BOW AND ARROW 🎯 TARGET

 SHOOTING
There are men's and women's events, as well as mixed ones. Athletes who have a physical disability can participate in this discipline.

👤 INDIVIDUAL 🔫 WEAPON 🎯 TARGET

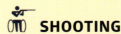 WHEELCHAIR RUGBY
Teams include both men and women. It is played by athletes who have a physical-motor disability.

👥 TEAM 🏉 BALL

 Scan this QR code to learn more about the **Paralympic Games**. http://mod.lk/oly_p

THE WINTER PARALYMPIC GAMES

Sports included in the Pyeongchang 2018 Winter Paralympic Games

BIATHLON
This discipline combines cross-country skiing and rifle shooting. Athletes who have a physical disability or visual impairments can participate in this event.

 INDIVIDUAL   SKI   RIFLE

ALPINE SKIING
This includes five disciplines: downhill, super-G, giant slalom, slalom, and super combined. Athletes who have a physical disability or visual impairments can participate in this event.

INDIVIDUAL   SKI

CROSS-COUNTRY SKIING
This is one of the sports that have featured in the Paralympic Games since its first edition. Athletes who have a physical disability or visual impairments participate in this discipline.

INDIVIDUAL   TEAM   SKI

ICE HOCKEY
 This is played by athletes who have a physical-motor disability.

 TEAM   STICK   PUCK

SNOWBOARD
Athletes who have a physical-motor disability compete in two disciplines: snowboard-cross and banked slalom.

 INDIVIDUAL   SNOWBOARD

WHEELCHAIR CURLING
There are mixed teams. It is played by athletes who have a physical-motor disability.

 TEAM   STONE   BROOM

23

ATHLETES

Until 1988, athletes participating in the Olympic Games were not allowed to be professionals, which meant they could not be associated with federations, nor could they be paid for competing. For this reason, many athletes could not attend the competitions, as they had neither financial resources nor support from their governments. Besides, most of the time they were unable to take time off of work to participate in the Games. With the rapid development of sports and the demand for better results, professional athletes were included in the competitions. Differently from the others, they were dedicated exclusively to sports. Today, the Games bring together the true elite of each discipline.

The fastest man alive

→ Jamaican athlete **Usain Bolt** is currently "the fastest man in the world": he won the 100 m, 200 m, and the 4 x 100 m relay in Beijing 2008; then he repeated this achievement in London 2012. He has now a total of eight gold medals in athletics!

Before Bolt, there were other great athletics Olympic medalists: American **Carl Lewis** won nine gold medals and one silver medal (Los Angeles 1984, Seoul 1988, Barcelona 1992, and Atlanta 1996). Finnish athlete **Paavo Nurmi** won nine gold medals and three silver medals (Antwerp 1920, Paris 1924, and Amsterdam 1928). Czech **Emil Zátopek** won three races in Helsinki 1952: 5,000 m, 10,000 m, and the marathon. His feat has never been surpassed. By that time, he had already won a gold and a silver medals in London 1948.

The greatest Olympic champion

→ American swimmer **Mark Spitz** was the first to win seven gold medals in one competition (Munich 1972). But his fellow countryman **Michael Phelps** surpassed him with six gold medals and two bronze medals at the Athens 2004 Olympics. Once again, in Beijing 2008, he won medals in all eight categories in which he competed, but this time they were all gold medals. He is the greatest Olympic champion: 28 medals in four editions, 23 of them being gold medals!

18 MEDALS

Most prominent Olympic *gymnasts*

● Soviet gymnast **Larisa Latynina** won 18 Olympic medals between 1956 and 1964, a record only broken by Michael Phelps. She is the woman who has won the most Olympic medals of all time. Another Soviet gymnast who made history in the Olympic Games was **Nikolai Andrianov**: he won 15 medals between 1972 and 1980! Romanian gymnast **Nadia Comaneci** achieved the perfect score, three gold medals, one silver medal, and one bronze medal when she was only 14 years old, in Montreal 1976! In Moscow 1980, she won two gold medals and two silver medals.

Brasileirinho

● Brazilian gymnast **Daiane dos Santos** did not win medals in Athens 2004 nor in Beijing 2008. However, she made history in the Olympic Games by performing Arabian double front somersaults, a floor exercise which became known as "Dos Santos". This took place in Athens 2004, to the sound of the song "Brasileirinho".

Basketball stars

● In Barcelona 1992, the USA basketball team was known as the "Dream Team". It included stars like **Michael Jordan** and **Magic Johnson** and secured the gold medal. But even before the Dream Team's achievements, Jordan had already won a gold medal in Los Angeles 1984; he is considered the best basketball player of all time. Johnson became an icon for his incredible performance on the court and for announcing, shortly before the Games, he was HIV positive.

● Brazilian **Oscar Schmidt** never won an Olympic gold medal, but he is the player who has scored the most points in the history of Olympic basketball: 1,093 points in five editions! In Seoul 1988, he scored 55 points against Spain: the best single-game scoring of all time. This record has not yet been broken.

American boxer **Muhammad Ali** won the gold medal in 1960 at the age of 18. The athlete later said he threw his medal into a river after having been the subject of discrimination at a restaurant in his hometown (Louisville, USA) because of the color of his skin.

Tarzan!

American athlete **Johnny Weissmuller** won three gold medals in swimming and a bronze medal in water polo in 1924. In 1928, he won two more gold medals in swimming. In 1932, he left his career in sports and started a new one as an actor. Two other American athletes followed his steps in the pursuit of a cinematography career: **Herman Brix**, silver medalist in shot-put weight in 1928, and **Glenn Morris**, gold medalist in the 1936 decathlon. Coincidentally, the three former Olympic athletes played the same character on the big screen: Tarzan.

Interesting facts

The youngest athlete to win an Olympic medal was **Henry Clundey**: he was the silver medalist in rowing in Stockholm 1912, at the age of 10!

Swedish shooter **Oscar Swahn** was the oldest Olympic athlete to win a medal. In 1920, at the age of 72, he won the silver medal in team double shot running deer contest. He had already won two gold medals and a bronze medal in London 1908, as well as a gold medal and a bronze medal in Stockholm 1912. He competed against his son, **Alfred Swahn**, in all the Olympic editions in which he participated.

In Paris 1924, British athlete **Eric Liddell** decided not to compete in the 100-m race because the event would be held on a Sunday, which is considered a sacred day according to his religion. He won the bronze medal in the 200 m and the gold medal in the 400 m. His story, and that of the 1924 British delegation, was told in the movie *Chariots of Fire*.

Ukrainian **Sergey Bubka** is synonymous with the pole vault. He won a gold medal in Seoul 1988 and set the world record from 5.83 m to 6.14 m, broken only in 2014 by French athlete **Renaud Lavillenie**.

6.14 m
5.83 m

German tennis player **Steffi Graf** is a tennis icon. She was the only woman to have won the Golden Slam: she won four Grand Slam titles and a gold Olympic medal in 1988. She also won a bronze medal in Seoul 1988 (in the doubles competition) and a silver medal in Barcelona 1992.

American **Edward Eagan** is the only athlete to win a gold medal in both the Summer Games (in boxing in 1920) and the Winter Games (in bobsleigh in 1932).

In Moscow 1980, German twins **Bernd** and **Jörg Landvoigt** won a gold medal in rowing. Other twins, Soviet athletes **Nikolay** and **Yuriy Pimenov**, came in second. The Landvoigt twins had also won a gold medal in Montreal 1976 and a bronze medal in Munich 1972.

Brazilian triple jumper **Adhemar Ferreira da Silva** won gold medals in Helsinki 1952 and in Melbourne 1956. At the end of the triple jump competition in Helsinki, he received an ovation from the public while he was running around the stadium and waving. The victory lap was born.

Outstanding Brazilians

- Brazilians who have won the most medals are sailing athletes. **Torben Grael** won five medals (gold in Atlanta 1996 and Athens 2004, silver in Los Angeles 1984, and bronze in Seoul 1988 and Sydney 2000). **Robert Scheidt** has five medals too: gold in Atlanta 1996 and Athens 2004, silver in Sydney 2000 and Beijing 2008, and bronze in London 2012. The sailing team has brought 18 medals to Brazil!
- These two sailors are followed by swimmer **Gustavo Borges**: silver in Barcelona 1992 and Atlanta 1996 and bronze in Atlanta 1996 and Sydney 2000.
- Judo is the Olympic discipline in which Brazil has won the most medals: 22 in total! Among the judo athletes are **Aurélio Miguel** (gold in Seoul 1988 and bronze in Atlanta 1996), **Rogério Sampaio** (gold in Barcelona 1992), and **Sarah Menezes** (the first Brazilian to win a women's judo gold medal, in London 2012).

> **Lars Grael**, Torben Grael's brother, won the bronze medal in Seoul 1988 and Atlanta 1996. In 1998, he was involved in an accident and had his right leg amputated. He returned to compete in sailing a few years later.

- Brazilian athlete João Carlos de Oliveira, known as **João do Pulo**, *was one of the promises in Montreal 1976 because he held the world record in long jump, but he only got the bronze medal. In Moscow 1980, he brought home another bronze medal. A year later, he had a car accident and lost his right leg.*

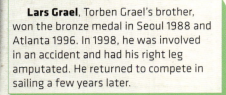

- In Athens 2004, a former Irish priest invaded the marathon and dragged Brazilian athlete **Vanderlei Cordeiro de Lima** off the road. The athlete, who was leading the race, finished in third, but won the Pierre de Coubertin special medal for his sportsmanship and Olympic spirit.

FAIR PLAY AND OLYMPIC SPIRIT

- In Tokyo 1964, Swedish brothers **Lars Gunnar Käll** and **Stig Lennart Käll** quit the sailing competition to help their opponents, whose boat had sunk. They won the first IOC Fair Play award. In Seoul 1988, Canadian sailor **Lawrence Lemieux** did the same, giving up the silver medal. He won a special prize from the IOC: the Pierre de Coubertin medal.
- In the Lillehammer 1994 Winter Games, a bobsleigh team was formed by four Croats, a Serb, and two Bosnians. Meanwhile, their countries were fighting in the Bosnian War.

Overcoming difficulties

In the history of the Olympics, there are many stories of overcoming adversities, especially regarding physical limitations.

- In Los Angeles 1984, American naturalized Swiss marathoner **Gabriela Andersen-Schiess** staggered the last 400 meters of the competition. As she crossed the line, she fainted and shocked the world.

- Many athletes competed while they were injured (they had a broken thumb or collarbone, for instance), but it was Danish athlete **Lis Hartel** who really overcame her physical limitations: in 1952 and 1956, when the Paralympic Games still had not been created, she won the silver medal in the equestrian competition after suffering from poliomyelitis during her pregnancy. She was paralyzed below her knees.

Danish athlete Lis Hartel had to be assisted by the champion Henri Saint Cyr to climb the podium.

- During the Turin 2006 Winter Games, the ski pole of Canadian skiing athlete **Sara Renner** broke. Norwegian coach **Bjørnar Håkensmoen** lent her one of his own. His attitude helped the Canadian get the silver medal, while Norway finished fourth.

Royalty also goes to the Olympics

- In Amsterdam 1928, the then Norwegian Prince **Olav V** won a gold medal with his sailing team.

- In Munich 1972, the former King of Spain, **Juan Carlos**, competed in sailing, but did not win. In Barcelona 1992, his son, Prince **Felipe de Bourbon**, also competed and did not win a medal either.

- In Rome 1960, the Greek sailing team won a gold medal. Team members included Prince **Constantine II** and his sister, Queen **Sofia** of Spain, acting as substitutes.

- In London 2012, equestrian athlete **Zara Phillips**, granddaughter of Queen Elizabeth II of England, won the silver medal in equestrian/eventing. Her mother, Princess **Anne**, also competed in the same discipline in Montreal 1976, but did not win a medal. Her father, **Mark Phillips**, won a gold medal in Munich 1972 and a silver medal in Seoul 1988.

MEMORABLE STORIES

- British athlete **Derek Redmond** suffered a leg injury during the 400 m competition in Barcelona 1992, but he did not accept medical assistance and continued in the competition, limping the remaining 150 m. His father ran onto the track and embraced him, helping him finish the race. It was one of the most touching moments in the history of the Games.

- At the age of 19, American athlete **Elizabeth Robinson**, who was a 1928 gold and silver medalist, was involved in a plane crash. She spent two months in a coma and two years unable to walk, but in 1936 she won the gold medal in the 4 x 100 m relay.

- Brazilian athlete **Adalberto Cardoso** ran barefoot in 1932, but did not win a medal. In 1960, Ethiopian athlete **Abebe Bikila** did the same and won a gold medal in the marathon. In Tokyo 1964, he won another gold medal, but this time he was wearing sneakers.

- Hungarian military **Károly Takács** lost his right hand in 1938 because of a grenade. After that, he had to train to compete in archery only with his left hand. He did it and won a gold medal in London 1948 and Helsinki 1952.

- Hungarian water polo athlete **Olivér Halassy** had a leg amputated during his childhood due to a streetcar accident. However, he won three gold medals (Amsterdam 1928, Los Angeles 1932, and Berlin 1936), despite the fact that the Paralympic Games had not yet been created.

- Portuguese athlete **Carlos Lopes** was run over two weeks before the Los Angeles 1984 Olympics. He recovered and competed in the Games, winning the gold medal in the marathon at the age of 37.

- In Atlanta 1996, American gymnast **Kerri Strug** had her ankle injured during her first vault, but she did not give up and made a perfect second vault, despite the intense pain.

- In Seoul 1988, American athlete **Greg Louganis** hit his head on the springboard during the diving competition. He was given five stitches and returned to the pool, winning two gold medals. Years later, he declared that he was HIV positive and that he was told so six months before the Games. By that time, he had already won two gold medals in Los Angeles 1984 and a silver medal in Montreal 1976.

CHEATING AND DOPING

- In 1904, American athlete **Fred Lorz** won the marathon, but was found to have completed part of the race by car! He was suspended from athletics, but was forgiven months later.

- In Berlin 1936, under the hegemony of Adolf Hitler, Germany was supposed to win the highest number of medals at any cost. For this reason, when German **Toni Merkens** was penalized for an illegal maneuver against Dutch **Arie van Vliet** in a cycling competition, he was fined 100 German marks, instead of losing his gold medal.

- After the fall of the Berlin Wall, some athletes who had participated in the Berlin 1936 Games admitted having been victims of doping by the government in order to improve their performance.

- In Rome 1960, Danish cyclist **Knud Jensen** fell unconscious and died during the competition due to the use of amphetamines. Since then, the IOC has been taking different measures to prevent and penalize athletes for doping. In Mexico 1968, strict control and drug tests started to be used in the Games.

- In Montreal 1976, modern pentathlon athlete **Boris Onischenko**, from the former Soviet Union, installed on his sword a system that gave him points without touching his opponent. When this was discovered, he was expelled from the Games and the sport.

- Brazilian long jump athlete **Maurren Maggi** could not participate in Athens 2004 because she was serving a doping suspension. She participated in Beijing 2008 and won a gold medal.

- In the Paralympic Games, in addition to medical analyses, there is a limit to the use of prosthetic or orthotic devices in each discipline in order to avoid technological doping.

- In Seoul 1988, Jamaican-born naturalized Canadian athlete **Ben Johnson** won the gold medal in the 100 m, defeating USA idol **Carl Lewis**, but it was later discovered that Johnson had taken a banned anabolic steroid. He had to return his medal and was suspended from the Games for two years. In Barcelona 1992, he did not make it to the semifinals.

SPORTS AND THE FUTURE

As technology has advanced, sports equipment has evolved a lot, offering athletes more safety as well as convenience.

➡️ **Arbitration** Technology has contributed to improving the work of judges, referees, and technical reviewers, providing resources such as sensors and measuring devices, among other media, to avoid mistakes in arbitration. One of the most important advances was photo finish, which appeared in 1932 to ensure results through images. Since then, much has evolved. Today, photos and videos are used to check the results, and there are even 3-D versions available.

➡️ **Athletics** There have been many developments in athletics. In 1988, carbon fiber poles were used for the first time. Until then, they were made of bamboo or wood, which meant more risks for the athletes. Nowadays, fiberglass poles are also an option.

Until 1964, **athletic tracks** were built using dust, sand, or coal dust. In Tokyo 1968, a synthetic track was used for the first time.

➡️ **Cycling** The year of 1937 was quite important for this sport: the first **bikes** with gears were ridden. By 1980, they were made of steel and, by the end of the 1990s, they were made of aluminum and carbon fiber.
In Athens 1986, bikes weighed about 16 kg; today, they weigh less than 7 kg.

Scan this QR code to learn more about **Olympic athletes**.
http://mod.lk/athletes

- **Fencing** Swords connected to electrical sensors were used for the first time in 1956, in order to facilitate identification of touching between fencers.

- **Skiing** Until 1972, the skis used during the Winter Games were made of wood. Today, they are made of a wood base and fiberglass.

- **Resources** Some athletes try to balance their physical limitations by using different resources, like Brazilian athlete Joaquim Cruz, who wore a 2-cm heel lift inside one of his sneakers to compensate for the difference in the length of his legs.

- **Horse riding** In this equestrian competition, the main "equipment" is the horse, and its performance is decisive for the results. In Sydney 2000, Brazilian Rodrigo Pessoa's horse, named Baloubet du Rouet, refused to jump an obstacle and they were eliminated. In Athens 2004, both won the silver medal, but the horse of Irish Cian O'Connor, who came in first place, was tested positive for doping, so Pessoa and Baloubet received the gold medal. In Beijing 2008, it was Pessoa's horse, Rufus, that did not pass the drug test, and they were eliminated from the competition.

- **Swimming** The most important development in this discipline was the fabric of **swimsuits**, which changed from Lycra™ to LZR, a technology developed by NASA. Nowadays, there are also swimsuits modeled on shark skin. Due to the difficulty in measuring the benefits of these swimsuits, they have been banned since 2010. As of 2012, pools have been equipped with a system that prevents the formation of waves when swimmers move.

During water testing in synchronized swimming, speakers are installed underwater so athletes can hear the music at all times.

33

BRAZIL
in the Games

In **1920**, Brazil participated in the Olympic Games for the first time. Brazilian athletes competed in five disciplines: swimming, rowing, water polo, diving, and shooting. It was in Antwerp, Belgium. Since then, Brazil has only missed the 1928 edition in Amsterdam, due to the economic hardship the country was going through. In Paris 1924, Los Angeles 1932, and Berlin 1936, Brazil did not win any medals.

→ To get to Antwerp 1920, the Brazilian athletes—who had been chosen just ten days before the Games—were traveling by ship to Lisbon when they realized they were not going to make it to the Games in time for the opening ceremony.

They traveled from there to the host city by train, in an open wagon, and it rained all the way to their destination.

When they arrived in Antwerp, they learned the competition had been postponed for a week. Despite the luck they had had, the archery team was robbed in Brussels. The athletes were only able to compete thanks to the American delegation, which lent them the necessary equipment.

In the end, Brazilian athletes brought home three medals: one gold, one silver, and one bronze, all won in **shooting** competitions.

The first South American woman to participate in the Games was Brazilian swimmer Maria Lenk, in Los Angeles 1932. She was only 17 years old.

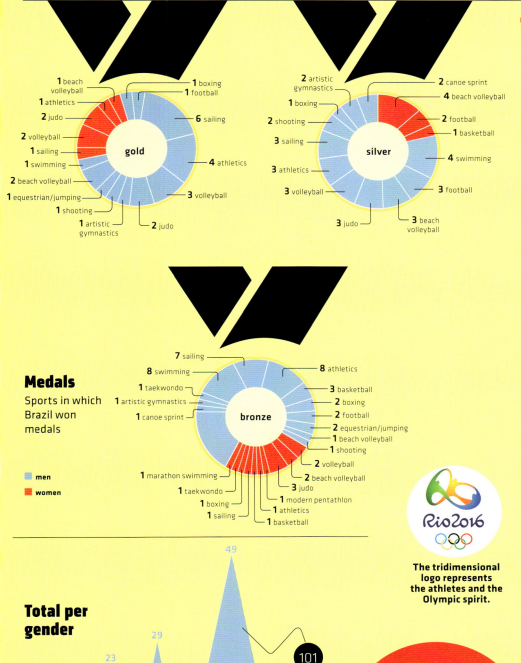

Medals
Sports in which Brazil won medals

- men
- women

Total per gender

- men
- women

The Games
IN BRAZIL

➤ On October 2, 2009, **Rio de Janeiro** was chosen over Tokyo, Chicago, and Madrid to be the host city of the 2016 Summer Games. The Olympic Games were held from August 5 to August 21, while the Paralympic Games were held from September 7 to September 18. For that reason, the city prepared a project to meet the IOC requirements regarding infrastructure: sports facilities for training and competitions, athletes' lodgings, air and ground transportation, accommodations and security, among other requirements. A team worked hard to offer the best possible Olympic experience to the world's top athletes.

➤ Fifteen Olympic disciplines, as well as eleven Paralympic disciplines, were present in the **Olympic Park**. Around 12,000 athletes stayed in the Olympic Village's 48 buildings, which are up for sale. There were about 60,000 volunteers working, including many from other countries.

➤ During the Rio 2016 Games, 32 disciplines were disputed.

The tridimensional logo represents the athletes and the Olympic spirit.

Scan this QR code to learn more about **Brazil in the Olympic Games.**
http://mod.lk/oly_pbr

➤ Archery competitions took place at the **Sambódromo**, Rio's venue for Carnival parades. It also hosted the finish line for the marathon. The **Maracanã Stadium** hosted the opening and closing ceremonies, as well as some of the football matches.

35

QUIZ

1 **Write at least five:**

a water sports

b two-player sports

c sports that require equipment

d winter sports

2 **Find the answers to these questions.**

a What sports are played exclusively by women?

b What sports are played exclusively by men?

c What sports can be played by mixed teams?

3 **Write five sports played both in the Summer Olympics and in the Summer Paralympic Games.**

4 **Write the questions to the following answers.**

a

Athletes must be between 15 and 18 years old.

b

The following sports: boating, tug-of-war, cricket, croquet, palm game, lacrosse, Basque pelota, polo, racquetball, and roque.

c

They are called pictograms.

5 Mention at least two differences between the opening and closing ceremonies at the Olympics.

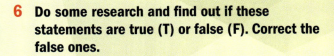

6 Do some research and find out if these statements are true (T) or false (F). Correct the false ones.

a ☐ Boxer's gloves can only be white or blue.
_____

b ☐ Pole vault athletes can choose the height, weight, and diameter of the pole.
_____
_____

c ☐ In badminton, athletes use two rackets and a small ball.
_____
_____

d ☐ Judokas can only wear white or blue *judogis* (judo uniforms).
_____
_____

e ☐ Judo judges must be black-belt *judokas*.
_____
_____

f ☐ In modern pentathlon, athletes must swim butterfly stroke.
_____
_____

Beyond the OLYMPIC GAMES

1 Find out about the attack on the Israeli delegation at the 1972 Munich Olympics and discuss with your History teacher: what were the reasons for that attack?

2 Why were there boycotts in the 1980 Games in Moscow and in the 1984 Games in Los Angeles? Do some research and answer.

3 Corruption problems tarnished the International Olympic Committee's image during the 1996 Atlanta Summer Games and the 2002 Salt Lake City Winter Games. Find out more about what happened and what the consequences were.

4 During the 1936 Berlin Olympic Games, something happened in the athletics competition that angered Adolf Hitler. What happened? Why did his attitude reflect that particular historical moment?

5 In 1968, American athletes Tommie Smith and John Carlos protested against racism. What was the event that motivated them to do that? What was the situation of African-Americans in the USA then?

6 What happened in Brazil in 1928 that prevented athletes from attending the Amsterdam Olympic Games?

37

Richmond

Direção editorial: Sandra Possas
Edição executiva de inglês: Izaura Valverde
Edição executiva de produção e multimídia: Adriana Pedro de Almeida
Coordenação de arte: Raquel Buim
Coordenação de revisão: Rafael Spigel

Edição de texto: Giuliana Gramani
Tradução: Ianina Zubowicz
Revisão: Carolina Waideman, Flora Vaz Manzione, Katia Gouveia Vitale, Márcio Martins, Marina Gomes, Ray Shoulder
Projeto gráfico: Hulda Melo
Edição de arte: David Urbinatti Netto, Hulda Melo, Marina Prado
Capa: Amanda Miyuki, Manuel Miramontes
Desenhos especiais: Eduardo Asta, Iansã Negrão, Inara Negrão, Ivan Luiz
Ilustrações: Guilherme D'arezzo
Iconografia: Márcia Sato, Sara Alencar
Coordenação de *bureau*: Rubens M. Rodrigues
Tratamento de imagens: Arleth Rodrigues, Bureau São Paulo, Luiz Carlos Costa, Marina M. Buzzinaro, Resolução Arte e Imagem
Pré-impressão: Alexandre Petreca, Everton L. de Oliveira Silva, Fabio N. Precendo, Hélio P. de Souza Filho, Marcio H. Kamoto, Rubens M. Rodrigues, Vitória Sousa

Embora todas as medidas tenham sido tomadas para identificar e contatar os detentores de direitos autorais sobre os materiais reproduzidos nesta obra, isso nem sempre foi possível. A editora estará pronta a retificar quaisquer erros dessa natureza assim que notificada.

Every effort has been made to trace the copyright holders, but if any omission can be rectified, the publishers will be pleased to make the necessary arrangements.

Impressão e acabamento: HRosa Gráfica e Editora
Lote: 292408

Créditos das fotos: Capa: Diego Barbieri/Shutterstock, Denis Kuvaev/Shutterstock, Muzsy/Shutterstock, Chen WS/Shutterstock, Diego Barbieri/Shutterstock, Radu Razvan/Shutterstock, Andrey Yurlov/Shutterstock, Melis/Shutterstock; pp. 2-3: Voropaev Vasiliy/Shutterstock, Clara/Shutterstock, IOC, Joe Scarnici/Getty Images, Ip Archive/Glow Images, Keystone-France/Gamma-Keystone/Getty Images, Thinkstock/Getty Images, Thinkstock/Getty Images, IOC, Walter Attenni/AP Photo/Glow Images, Dapd/AP Photo/Glow Images, AFP, Popperfoto/Getty Images; pp. 4-5: Dominique Mollard/AP Photo/Glow Images, Thinkstock/Getty Images, Locog/Zumapress/Glow Images; p. 6: IOC; p. 7: pôsteres: IOC, mascotes: TV-Yesterday/IT/Alamy/Glow Images, Martin Hoffmann/Imago Stock/Keystone Brasil, Sver Simon/Imago Stock/Keystone Brasil, Tony Duffy/Getty ImagesSport/Getty Images, Martin Hoffmann/Imago Stock/Keystone Brasil, Xavier Subias/Age Fotostock/Keystone Brasil, Gail Mooney/Corbis/Latinstock, Martin Hoffmann/Imago Stock/Keystone Brasil, Ulrich Baumgarten/Getty Images, IOC, IOC, IOC, IOC; p. 8: IOC; p. 9: IOC, IOC, IOC, Charlie Riedel/AP Photo/Glow Images; pp. 10-11: Xinhua/Eyevine/Glow Images, IOC, PhotoXpress/ZUMA PRESS/Glow Images, Daniel Swee/Alamy/Glow Images, IOC; pp. 12-13: Paul J Sutton/PCN/Corbis/Latinstock, IOC, IOC, Christian Petersen/AP Photo/Glow Images, IOC, IOC, Petr Toman/Shutterstock, IOC, IOC, IOC, IOC; pp. 14-17: IOC, IOC, IOC, PCN Photography/Alamy/Glow Images, IOC, IOC, Luca85/Shutterstock, IOC, IOC, IOC, IOC, IOC, Michael Weber/ImageBroker/Glow Images, IOC, IOC, PCN Photography/Alamy/Glow Images, IOC, IOC, IOC, Popperfoto/Getty Images, IOC, IOC, Christina Pahnke/Sampics/Corbis/Latinstock, IOC, IOC, IOC, IOC, Stefan Matzke/Sampics/Corbis/Latinstock, IOC, IOC, IOC, IOC, IOC, Popperfoto/Getty Images, IOC, IOC, IOC, IOC, IOC, IOC, Paul Gilham/Getty Images, IOC, IOC, IOC; pp. 18-19: Gregorio Borgia/AP Photo/Glow Images, IOC, IOC, IOC, IOC, IOC, PCN Photography/Alamy/Glow Images, IOC, IOC, IOC, IOC, PCN Photography/Alamy/Glow Images, IOC, IOC, IOC, Action Plus Sports Images/Alamy/Glow Images, IOC, The Canadian Press, Jonathan Hayward/AP Photo/Glow Images, IOC; p. 20: Andy Lyons/Getty Images, Bob Thomas/Getty Images, IOC; pp. 21-22: Action Plus Sports Images/Alamy/Glow Images, IOC, Action Plus Sports Images/Alamy/Glow Images, IOC, IOC, IOC, IOC, IOC, IOC, IOC, Leo Mason sports photos/Alamy/Glow Images, IOC, IOC, IOC, IOC, IOC, IOC, IOC, IOC, IOC, IOC, Thanassis Stavrakis/AP Photo/Glow Images; p. 23: Scott Hallenberg/Alamy/Glow Images, IOC, A3929/Julian Stratenschulte/dpa/Corbis, IOC, IOC, IOC, IOC, IOC, Martin Rose/Bongarts/Getty Images; pp. 24-33: Eric Lalmand/UPPA/ZUMA PRESS/Glow Images, PCN Photography/Alamy/Glow Images, RIA Novosti/Alamy/Glow Images, Keystone Pictures USA/Alamy/Glow Images, Ben Stansall/AFP, Hipólito Pereira/Agência O Globo, Susan Ragan/AP Photo/Glow Images, MixPix/Alamy/Glow Images, Photos 12 – Cinema/Archives du 7e Art/MGM/DR/Diomedia, 20th Century Fox/Courtesy/Getty Images, Mary Evans/Ronald Grant Archive/Diomedia, Topical Press Agency/Hulton Archive/Getty Images, Reprodução, Bob Thomas/Getty Images, Ben Radford/Getty Images, Ben Radford/Getty Images, Alexander Hassenstein/Getty Images, Jiro Mochizuki/AFP, Imago Stock/Keystone Brasil, Picture-Alliance/dpa/Other Images, Terry Fincher/Hulton Archive/Keystone/Getty Images, Agence Zoom/Getty Images, PCN Photography/Alamy/Glow Images, Romeo Gacad/AFP, Mister Shadow/dpa/Corbis/Latinstock, Thinkstock/Getty Images, Radu Razvan/Shutterstock, Gambarini Maurizio/Picture-Alliance/dpa/AP Photo/Glow Images; pp. 34-35: Abril Comunicações S/A, Rio 2016™.

Dados internacionais de Catalogação na Publicação (CIP)
(Câmara Brasileira do Livro, SP, Brasil)

Amendola, Roberta
  Learn about the olympic games / Roberta Amendola. – 2. ed. – São Paulo : Moderna, 2021.

  1. Esportes – Literatura infantojuvenil 2. Jogos olímpicos – História 3. Literatura infantojuvenil 4. Olimpíadas – História I. Título.

20-47147   CDD-028.5

Índices para catálogo sistemático:

1. Jogos olímpicos : História : Literatura infantojuvenil   028.5
2. Jogos olímpicos : História : Literatura juvenil   028.5

Maria Alice Ferreira – Bibliotecária – CRB-8/7964

ISBN 978-65-5779-531-6

Reprodução proibida. Art. 184 do Código Penal e Lei 9.610, de 19 de fevereiro de 1998.
Todos os direitos reservados.

RICHMOND
EDITORA MODERNA LTDA.
Rua Padre Adelino, 758 — Belenzinho
São Paulo — SP — Brasil — CEP 03303-904
www.richmond.com.br
2021

Impresso no Brasil

Este livro não é uma publicação oficial do COB ou do COI.